Nana's
TIPS FOR GRACIOUS LIVING

BY **NONA J. ZIMMERMAN**

DIAMOND KEY PRESS Edited by Charmain Zimmerman Brackett
Illustrations and design by Leonard "Porkchop" Zimmerman

Introduction

Fashion and trends change over the years, but good manners are always in style. When writing this book, I was reminded of a slower time, when there were no cell phones and when families actually sat down at supper time and talked about what happened that day.

Today things are so much faster. Everybody wants everything NOW.

Some of the etiquette tips in this book are pet peeves of mine. That's actually how the idea of the book was conceived. And while I'm not a writer like my daughter, these were still notes I wanted to share.

These are suggestions; a lot of them come from the school of hard knocks and are lessons I've learned along the way. Others are, or should be, just common knowledge and are grounded in showing kindness, thoughtfulness, and respect for others.

I hope you enjoy the illustrations and that they make you laugh. The diagrams shown here are how I do it, but if you do it differently that's all well and good. The hope is that these can help you out.

I'm sure I haven't covered them all, so consider this a living, breathing collection. We've left space to add more to the back of the book as you come across them!

I guess the main thing I want to convey is to show kindness, give a smile, and as my son would say, spread HAPPY.

Part *One*
GRACIOUS LIVING *at home*

When someone enters the room, always acknowledge them.

NANA'S TIPS FOR 6 GRACIOUS LIVING

Try to always offer a word of encouragement or give a compliment when possible. You never know what other people are going through. You might have just made their day.

Praise publicly; criticize privately.

NANA'S TIPS FOR 8 GRACIOUS LIVING

When people show you something on their phone, don't swipe to the left or right, you never know what's next.

NANA'S TIPS FOR 9 GRACIOUS LIVING

It isn't always necessary to correct. So what if they mispronounced a word? It will just embarrass them and doesn't make you look any bigger.

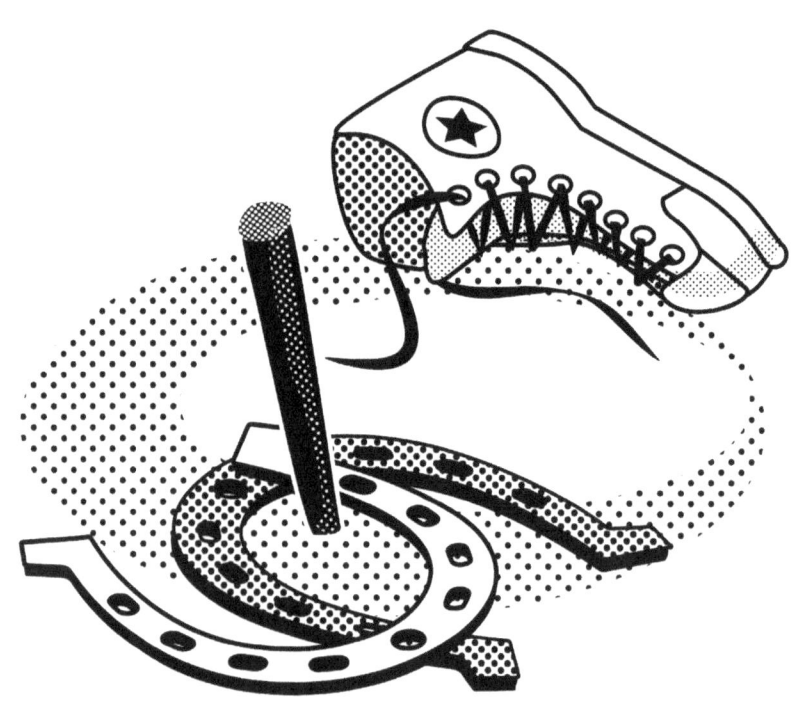

NANA'S TIPS FOR 10 GRACIOUS LIVING

If you borrow something, make sure you return it promptly and in same condition you borrowed it. Also, if you use something belonging to someone, be sure to return it to the spot it came from.

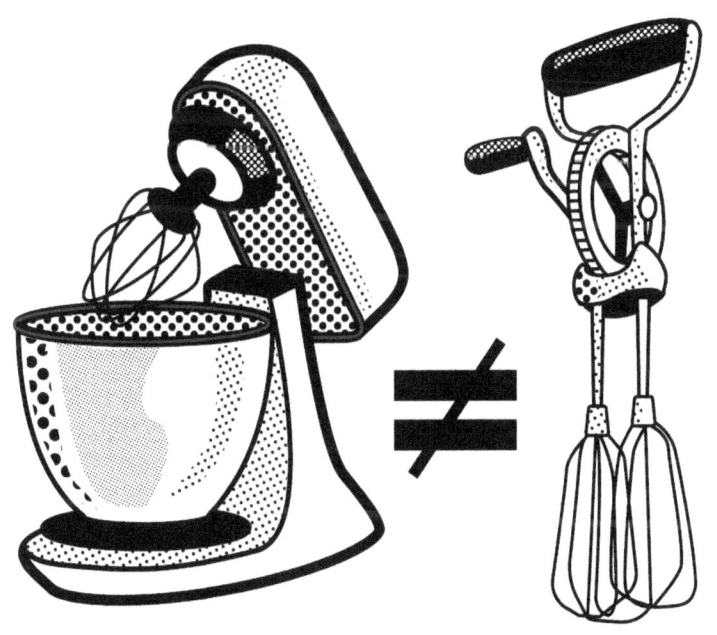

Item Borrowed **Item Returned**

NANA'S TIPS FOR GRACIOUS LIVING

It's hard to hear a nod.
My mother used to say she
couldn't tell if it was a "yes"
or "no" rattle. In the South,
we follow those words with
a "ma'am" or "sir."

Learn to turn the lights off when leaving a room. You will appreciate that lesson when you start paying the bills.

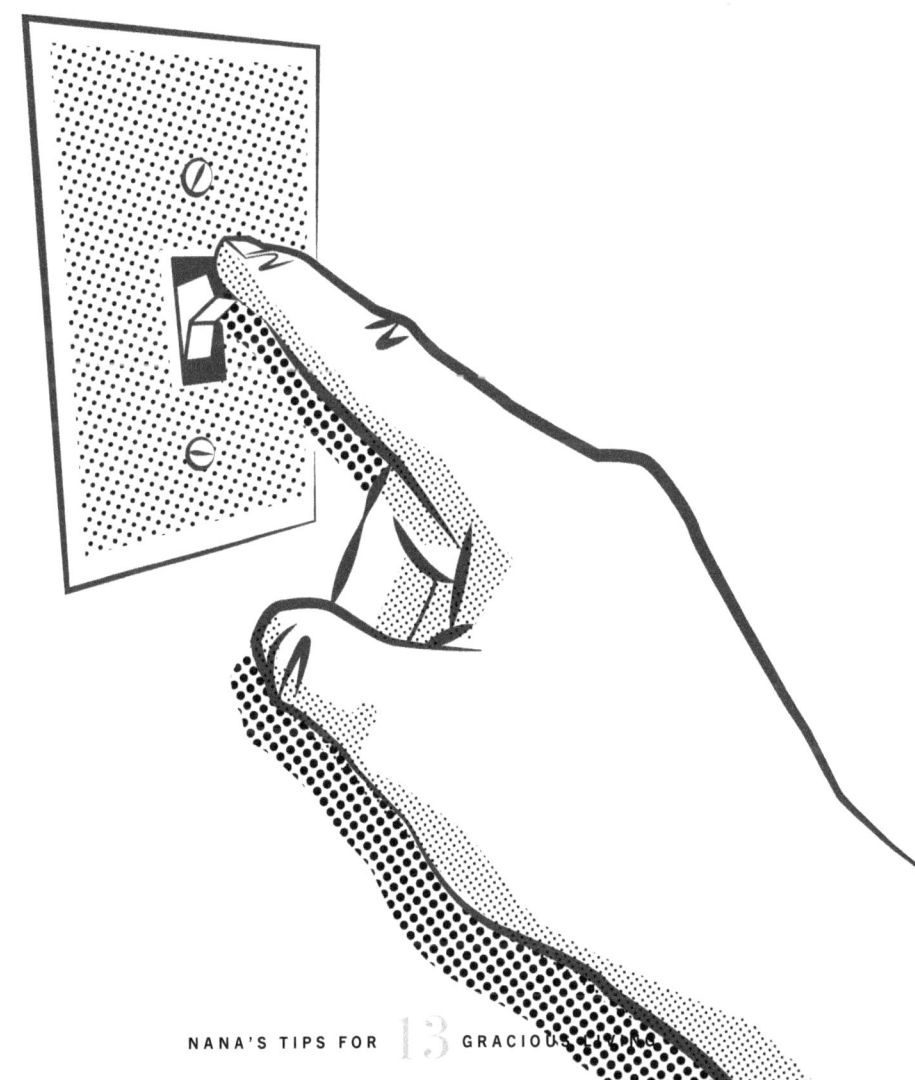

NANA'S TIPS FOR 13 GRACIOUS LIVING

If there is only one of something left, always ask if anyone else wants it or offer to split it.

NANA'S TIPS FOR GRACIOUS LIVING

And like my brother, Jimmy, always said, "If you've eaten so much you could pop, please don't pop at the table."

NANA'S TIPS FOR 15 GRACIOUS LIVING

Be careful not to interrupt someone else talking. Try to wait your turn, although when you get older you will try to hurry up before you forget what you were going to say.

Contrary to popular belief "bless your heart" isn't a polite insult. It's often used to show you care. If a person's car breaks down or someone loses a job, that's a great time to use the phrase.

Loud burping isn't very polite.

NANA'S TIPS FOR 18 GRACIOUS LIVING

When you receive a gift from someone or someone goes out of the way to do something nice for you, always show gratitude. Sometimes, I have had to sacrifice something I wanted or needed, in order to have the cash to purchase a gift. How disrespectful to not even be thanked! Your "thank you" can be a phone call, a text, an email. SEND THE THANK YOU NOTE!

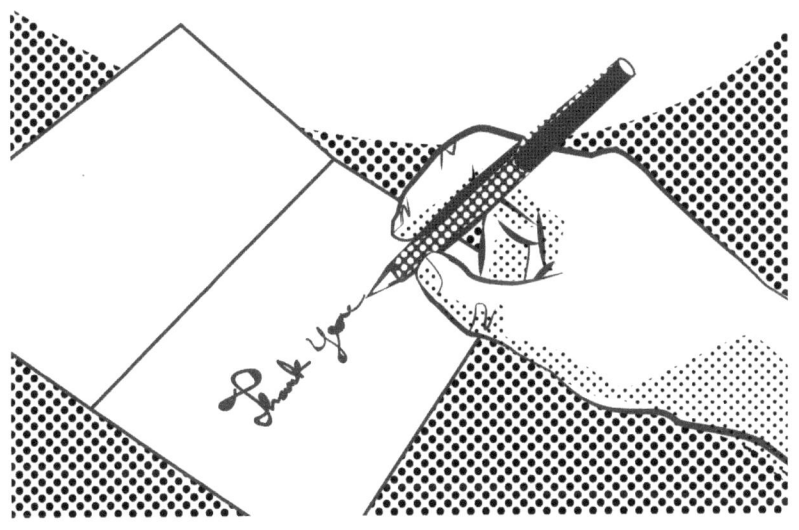

Everyone is different, and they all have hopes and dreams. A little bit of kindness can go a long way.

And if your Mama never told you, your Nana will, if you can't say anything nice, don't say anything at all.

NANA'S TIPS FOR 20 GRACIOUS LIVING

Remember your word is your bond. If you tell someone that you are going to do something, DO IT!

That person believed what you said and may have had to change plans. Things change and you may not be able to fulfill that promise; however, you should let the person know. Not to inform someone is rude and disrespectful.

Part *Two*

GRACIOUS LIVING
elsewhere

When dropping people off, make sure they are in their house safely before leaving.

NANA'S TIPS FOR 24 GRACIOUS LIVING

When you and someone else run into an acquaintance, introduce the person you are with first, this will usually give the acquaintance a chance to introduce themselves. (And if you're the type to forget names, it can help you out too.)

Respect other people and their belongings. Don't put your feet on furniture that does not belong to you. Don't let your child jump up and down on furniture, at someone's home, in a restaurant, etc. They could get hurt.

When visiting others, you should never bring your pet without permission.

When you are in traffic and someone is trying to get out of a parking lot, if it is safe, let them out.

When someone is kind enough to let you out in traffic, acknowledge it with a "thank-you" wave.

NANA'S TIPS FOR 29 GRACIOUS LIVING

Along the financial lines, if money is tight you might want to try something my husband and I did for anniversaries or other special occassions. We went to the store together, picked out a card we liked, handed it to each other, read it,

and then put in back on the shelf. It's the sentiment you share and saving a few bucks. No big deal, you were probably going to throw in trash eventually anyway. Hope money is never that tight for you, but if so, try this.

If you are shopping and have to step in front of someone else who is also shopping, say "excuse me."

NANA'S TIPS FOR 32 GRACIOUS LIVING

If you have a lot of items in the checkout line, and someone comes behind you with only a couple of items, let that person go ahead of you.

If you see someone struggling with bags, ask if you can help.

NANA'S TIPS FOR 34 GRACIOUS LIVING

When entering or exiting a building, hold the door for the person behind you.

NANA'S TIPS FOR 35 GRACIOUS LIVING

When walking near traffic, the most able-bodied person should walk closest to the traffic. In case, they need to quickly protect them.

When in public, try to keep your little ones under your control. We all get tired and so do the little ones who may start crying or have a temper tantrum. If this happens, take them outside until they can calm down. Some people will let their children scream and cry and ignore them. That might work for home but not in public.

If you are watching a video
or any media on your
cell phone, please use
headphones.

If your children play games
on your cell phone, either
let them use headphones
or mute it.

When out in public, do not use the speaker phone. It is disrespectful to those around you. If you are hard of hearing, ask the person calling to wait and step outside.

NANA'S TIPS FOR 10 GRACIOUS LIVING

One of the saddest things I've witnessed is to be at a restaurant or somewhere there is family sitting around the table, and they are all looking at their phones. You have family come over and again instead of talking to one another, they are all looking at their phones. There should be a "check your phone" at the door.

When someone else is paying the restaurant bill, avoid selecting the most expensive thing on the menu.

NANA'S TIPS FOR 12 GRACIOUS LIVING

On Credit Cards – a good rule to follow is not to charge more than you are able to pay each month. If you only are making a payment, you are not getting anywhere as the interest that is being charged each month will sometimes eat up the payment you made.

Each year, I get a wall calendar and go through the year recording my family or friend's birthday or an anniversary. Then at the end of the month, I check the following month to see who has a birthday or an anniversary. I get a card, address it, sign it and put a stamp on it, put a sticky note on the card showing when I should mail it. Your friends will think you have a wonderful memory.

I learned this trick many years ago when I was a beauty consultant with Mary Kay. I always asked those in attendance to write their birthdays on a paper I had given them, just the month and day (no year). Then on their birthday, I would send them a card.

QUESTIONS TO AVOID

"When is your baby due?" unless you know for a fact that a woman is pregnant.

"When are you getting married?" to your single friends.

"When are you going to start a family?" to couples of any age.

And never ask an older woman how old she is, unless you want to get popped in the head. I knew a very famous person that once said, "A woman that will tell her age, will tell anything."

Part Three

Nana's How I Do

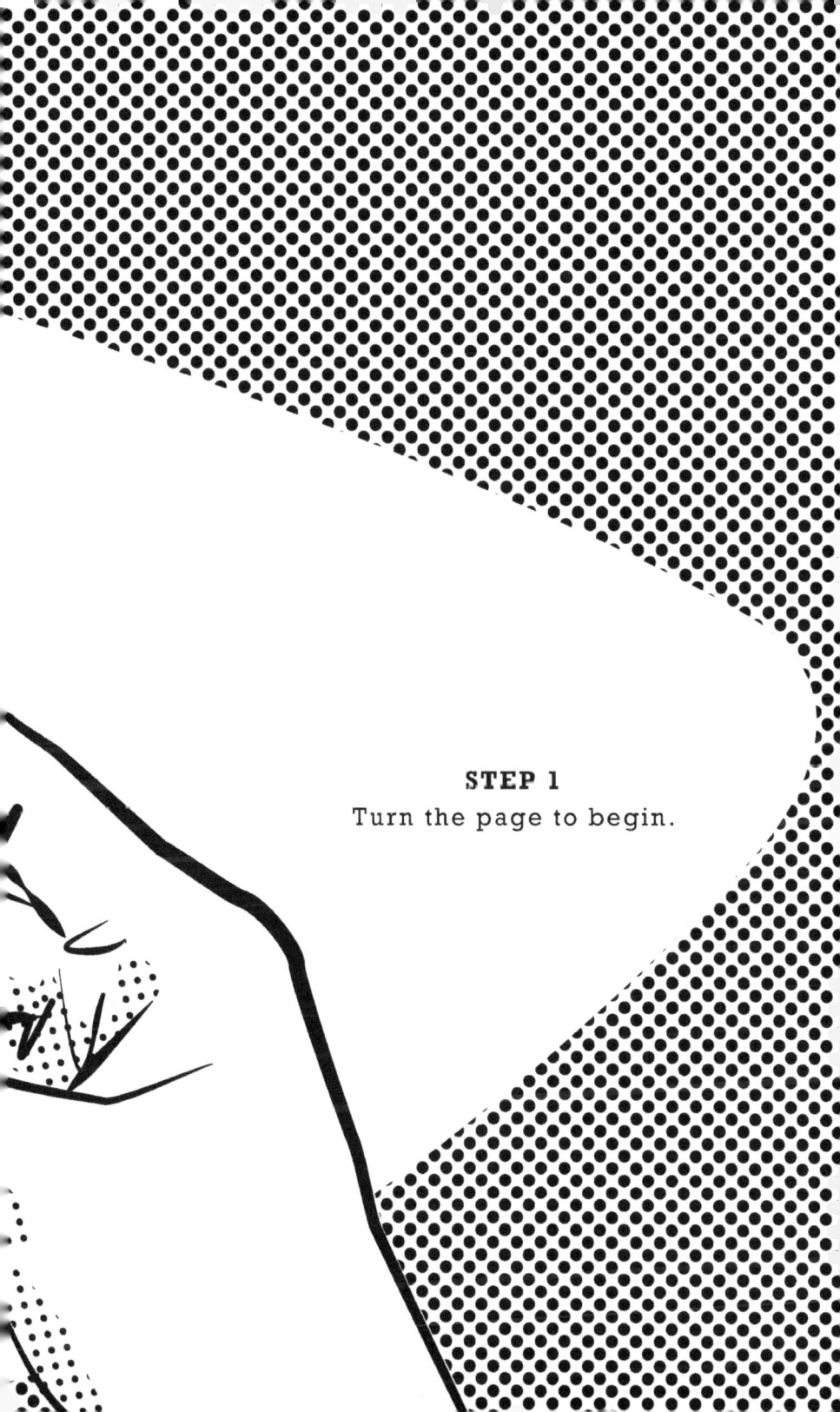

HOW I: *Set the table*

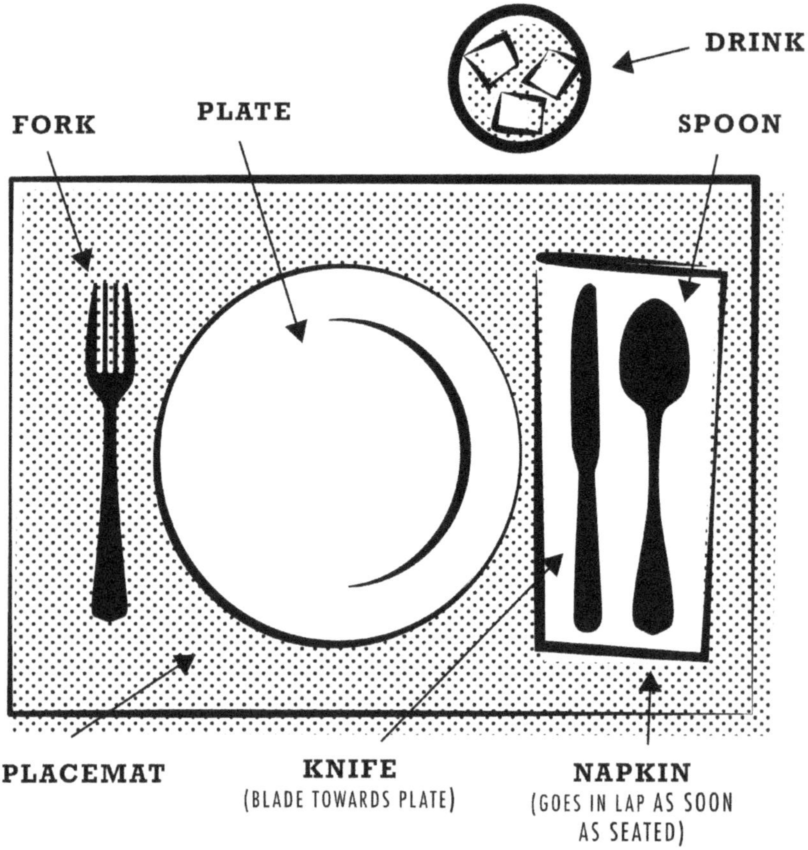

DRINK

FORK

PLATE

SPOON

PLACEMAT

KNIFE
(BLADE TOWARDS PLATE)

NAPKIN
(GOES IN LAP AS SOON AS SEATED)

If you end up somewhere with more utensils than I've shown you here, start from the furthest out and work inward... or just watch to see what someone else does.

NANA'S TIPS FOR 50 GRACIOUS LIVING

HOW I: *Make a tomato sandwich*

BREAD

TOMATO

MAYO

KNIFE

SALT & PEPPER

FIRST
Add Dukes* Mayonnaise to two pieces of bread (can be toasted)

*For delicious results

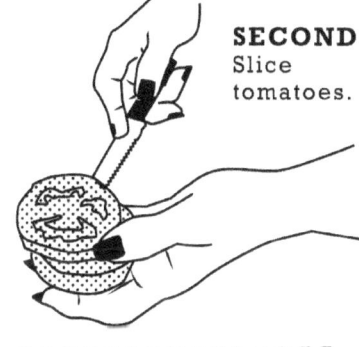

SECOND
Slice tomatoes.

THIRD
Add salt and pepper to taste.

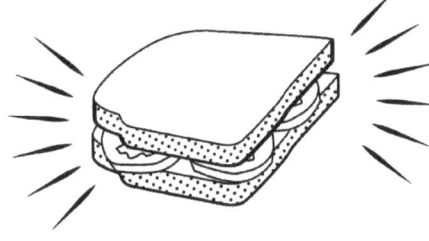

VIOLA!

PRO TIP

Summer, homegrown tomatoes make the best sandwiches.

You can also add bacon, lettuce, cheese, or ham, but it's better with just tomatoes.

HOW I: *Fold a fitted sheet*

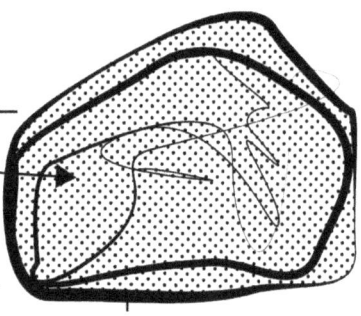

UNFOLDED FITTED SHEET
This one is easy when you realize that big wad of fabric is really just a squishy square.

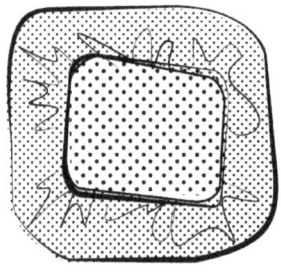

STEP 1
Unball the sheet and lay out with the elastic up.

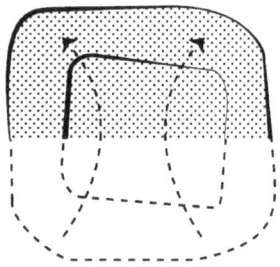

STEP 2
Fold bottom two corners up to match top two corner seams.

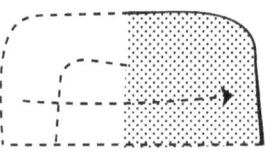

STEP 3
Fold that in half (with elastic inside).

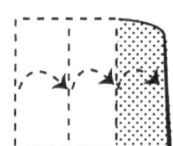

STEP 4
Fold that into a third. It's getting smaller fast.

LAST STEP
Fold it down into a square and you will impress your mother.

NANA'S TIPS FOR 52 GRACIOUS LIVING

HOW I: *Write a Thank You*

STEP 1
You can purchase or make your own "thank you" card.

STEP 2
Here's a sample of a "thank you" note.

The note doesn't have to be that long; however, you can always add personal lines, such as; "it was great to see you." "I'm so glad you were able to come" or whatever fits the occasion.

Dear RECIPIENT,

Just a note to thank you for GIFT RECEIVED. I know that it will be put to good use. You are always so thoughtful, and I appreciate it so much.

Again, thank you,
　　　　　YOUR NAME

STEP 3
Insert note into envelope and seal. Address to sender, add return address. Affix postage and drop in a mailbox.

PRO TIP

Your thank you doesn't have to be a handwritten note, it can be an email, text or telephone call, but for goodness sake, ***SEND THE DANG "THANK YOU."***

NANA'S TIPS FOR GRACIOUS LIVING

Thank You

I would like to thank my son, Leonard "Porkchop" Zimmerman, for his talent and sometimes patience in getting Nana's Tips for Gracious Living in production. Also, thanks to my daughter, Charmain Zimmerman Brackett for her editing skills in checking both my grammar and spelling. Both my children are so busy with their own projects but took the time to help me with mine.

I also would like to remember my sweet husband, Leonard Sr. He was always my biggest cheerleader and supported me in anything I undertook.

Special thanks to Bret, Jessica, Allie, Jeremy, and Ginger for helping me stay sane the last three years.

Also a big thank you to Ashlee Henry for coming to our aid, once again, with her help in the technical aspects of getting this together.